British Rail's Advanced Passenger Train owes much to the experimental APT-E
design seen here on the first main line run prior to starting the most stringent test
programme ever devised for a railway train.

The final APT prototype train, picture right, covered thousands of miles of vital
main line testing as a prelude to the entry into public service of this world leader in
railway passenger operation.

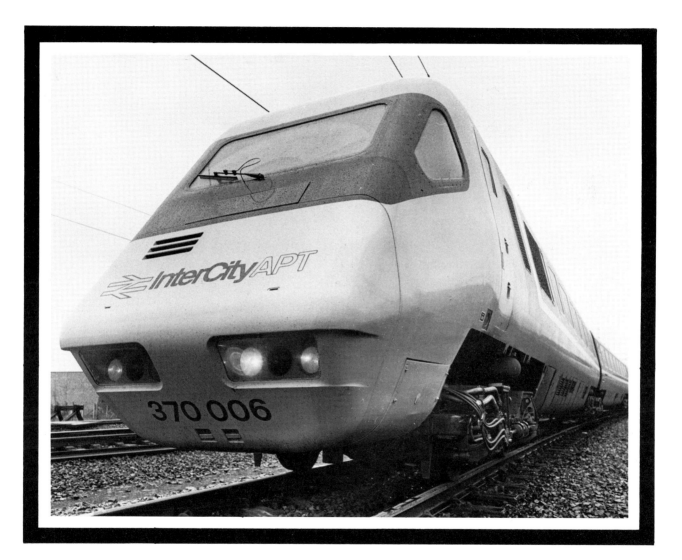

The Advanced Passenger Train is a major British railway engineering achievement. Its revolutionary features represent the culmination of years of imaginative research, planning, production and testing which have given Britain and British Rail a world lead in the sphere of fast and comfortable railway travel. This book has been published to herald the introduction of the APT to public service and seeks to describe and portray the new train and give an insight into the years of its evolution.

ISBN 0 905466 37 3 ©1981

Published by Avon-AngliA Publications & Services,
Annesley House, 21 Southside,
Weston-super-Mare, BS23 2QU.

In association with British Rail,
London Midland and Scottish Regions

Printed by H. G. Stone & Co. (Printers) Ltd,
Wymondham, Norfolk

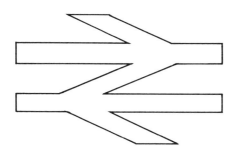

ADVANCED PASSENGER TRAIN

The official illustrations in this book are reproduced by courtesy of British Rail. Additional photographs were kindly supplied by R. Puntis Esq. The book has been compiled by Geoffrey Body MCIT in conjunction with the staff of the General Manager, BR (LMR), Euston.

Contents

High Speed Heritage . . . . page 6
The APT Story — A Summary 8
APT-E — The Experimental Period 10
Testing Time 16
Train Evolution and Description 21
Route Chart 24
Plans, Drawings and Diagrams 26
APT-P — Construction 32
Advanced Passenger Train in Action 34
Chronology 46

HIGH SPEED HERITAGE

Despite its curves and the steep gradients of the northern section, the West Coast route to Scotland has a tradition of high speeds dating back to the dramatic racing years at the end of the last century. On this page the Up Royal Scot is seen passing through Shap station headed by one of the 'Coronation' Pacifics introduced in 1937 and 6113 *Cameronian* climbs to Beattock with the Glasgow portion of the train in 1928.

High speeds have continued to be an important
factor in catering for passengers between London
and Glasgow. These scenes show 'Jubilee' class
4—6—0 45741 approaching Euston and two trains of
the diesel and electric era — with two Class 50
2700 hp diesels backing onto the Royal Scot at Crewe
and Class 87 5000 hp electric locomotive 87002
approaching Beattock on its way to Glasgow.

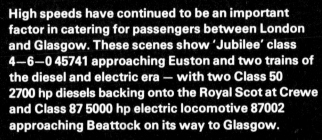

THE APT STORY— A SUMMARY

From the days of the Railway Race to the North and to Aberdeen at the end of the last century, through the record breaking years of the 1930s, the West Coast route to Scotland has maintained a tradition of fast passenger train services. The tradition continued with the advent of the 100 mph electrification era which reached the cities of the North West by 1967 and in 1974 was extended through to Glasgow. Now, as the 125 mph High Speed Train revolutionises services on the Western and Eastern Regions of British Rail, the West Coast main line remains in the forefront of modern railway development with the coming of the Advanced Passenger Train.

The Advanced Passenger Train (APT) has evolved over a lengthy and highly complex development period from two fundamental philosophies. The Inter-City passenger service concept of the British Railways Board called for the provision of shorter journey times with greater passenger comfort and without charging special fare supplements. In technical terms this meant producing a train which would take its part in the progressive replacement programme and also achieve higher speeds on existing track by tackling the problem of the abundance of curves to be found on most British main line routes.

From these starting points BR's Research & Development Division at Derby began a programme of fundamental research into the riding characteristics of railway vehicles. From this work, in turn, the unique tilting mechanism of the Advanced Passenger Train was developed.

The APT is an electrically-powered Inter-City train designed for a maximum speed of 155 mph but, most importantly, capable of tilting and thus allowing speeds through curves of between 20% and 40% higher than conventional trains and in complete safety and comfort. This capability means that the 401 mile Glasgow — London route can be covered by the APT in a scheduled time of 4 hours 15 minutes — an average of 94 mph.

The APT design programme began at the end of the 1960s and one major step was the construction of an experimental gas turbine powered train which during trials in 1975 reached 152 mph. On another test it cut the existing London — Leicester timing from 84 to 58 minutes — an average of 100 mph. Following this experimental work came a programme for constructing three new, prototype APT sets for the Glasgow — London route. These were designed by the British Railways Board's Chief Mechanical & Electrical Engineer and were built by British Rail Engineering Ltd at Derby.

Each train consists of 14 vehicles, with two 4000 hp power cars sandwiched between two identical articulated rakes of six passenger carrying vehicles. The attractive passenger environment is complemented by comfortable seating, double glazing and air conditioning with de-odorising carbon filters and sealing from external pressures. Catering cars provide a full meal service and buffet facilities. The passenger-controlled, power-operated sliding doors allow easy access to the coaches. The guard has overriding door control.

Extensive use of aluminium in the construction of the APTs, plus articulation of the coaches, means that weight is reduced and hence energy consumption kept to a minimum. The trains also have a novel hydrokinetic (water turbine) braking system which can dissipate the high energy levels involved and stop the train within the clearances of existing signalling. The higher speed limits permitted for APT are shown in the driver's cab by means of the C-APT system which relays information from transponders on the track. Another feature is the provision of chemical retention toilets.

The advanced technology and innovation incorporated in APT mean that the trains need to be maintained and serviced to a high standard. At the Glasgow end of the initial route the existing maintenance depot at Shields has been adapted for the APT requirement and the carriage servicing depot at Polmadie has had a special washing machine installed to clean the APT's unique profile. In London cleaning accommodation has been provided at Willesden. For major overhaul the APT will be returned to Derby. Particular attention has been paid to the training of operating, technical and catering staff assigned to the APT services.

After extensive trials, during which a record speed of 160 mph was achieved on 20 December 1979, the first regular 125 mph APT passenger service between Glasgow and Euston was scheduled to start in 1981 with a 255 minute timing. Ahead, in the mid-1980s, lies the prospect of a fleet of APTs for all the electrified West Coast main line services to the North West and West Midlands.

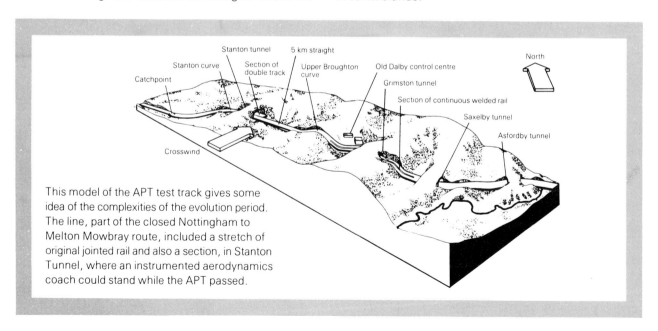

This model of the APT test track gives some idea of the complexities of the evolution period. The line, part of the closed Nottingham to Melton Mowbray route, included a stretch of original jointed rail and also a section, in Stanton Tunnel, where an instrumented aerodynamics coach could stand while the APT passed.

Labels on model: Catchpoint, Stanton curve, Stanton tunnel, Section of double track, 5 km straight, Upper Broughton curve, Old Dalby control centre, North, Grimston tunnel, Section of continuous welded rail, Saxelby tunnel, Asfordby tunnel, Crosswind

APT-E

By the middle of 1971 the APT project was moving away from the drawing board and model stage to the point at which hardware was arriving at the Advanced Projects Laboratory in the Railway Technical Centre at Derby for the building of full sized test vehicles. The APT-E trailer cars, pictured above, owed much of their design to aircraft industry techniques. This shows up in the other photograph where the articulation bogie is being linked to one of the skeletal cars in readiness for test towing.

THE EXPERIMENTAL PERIOD

The distinctive APT shape is already beginning to emerge in the picture (left) of one of the two power cars under construction at Derby for the four-car experimental train. Powered by eight 300 hp gas turbine engines, APT-E made its first run on 25 July 1972. The two-car test bed POP started proving the suspension, tilting and braking systems from September 1971 and by March 1973 — when it was captured in the picture (top) on the Melton Junction to Edwalton test track — had covered over 13,000 miles.

The pictures on this page show a multi-car APT-E unit outside the Railway Technical Centre at Derby and (below) at Melton Mowbray en route to the test track.

On the opposite page are two interior views, one of the driving cab and the other of the central instrumentation console. The APT-E was, to all intents and purposes, a full size mobile laboratory. The engineers at the console were able to register every parameter of suspension, traction, aerodynamics, braking, vehicle structure and ride characteristics for measurement and analysis.

The lower illustration shows Laboratory Coach 4 (Hastings). This was one of the narrow width vehicles from the SR Hastings route and was used for trials of the coach tilt system using a bogie design derived from the results of running APT-E. Tilted for the camera while waiting at signals before a test run, the air bag suspension unit can clearly be seen.

After over three years of useful life APT-E retired to the National Railway Museum at York in 1975 but not before it had produced a run of 152 mph and contributed a vast amount of information to the design of its successor, APT-P.

Following the decision to build three passenger carrying pre-production prototype trains, the first APT-P vehicle emerged from Derby Locomotive Works in June 1977.
By 1978 a power car and three trailers were undergoing commissioning trials.

TESTING TIME

A notable day
APT-P makes its
first run from Shields Depot
under its own power on
26 April 1979

On the same day APT-P is seen in the upper picture at Law Junction and, below, at Carstairs. This was the period of the Penmanshiel Tunnel blockage and the High Speed Train shuttle from Edinburgh stands at the opposite platform. The two trains make an interesting comparison in modern train design.

Passing Newton (Glasgow) on 10 February 1980
APT-P shows its tilting capacity. The lower scene is
at Larkfield Junction. Transclyde unit 303 012 is in
the foreground.

Amid the paraphernalia of electric current supply and colour light signalling, APT-P sets off from Glasgow Central on its first run to Euston. Above, the train is seen at Ravenstruther.

Like so much of recent technical innovation, the Advanced Passenger Train was born of the computer. Making light of calculations that would have taken mathematicians years the computer time available to BR's Research & Development Division produced a new understanding about the 'hunting' action of rail vehicle bogies and of the reactions between trains and the track on which they ran. The result was a capability for producing trains which could operate much faster than the 100 mph ceiling once considered the maximum.

Coinciding with these changes in technical understanding in the second half of the 1960s came a dramatic response in terms of passenger business to the first phase of electrification on the West Coast main line. The Japanese too had already found out that higher speeds meant more passengers but Britain had neither funds nor reason for building straight, new, speed tracks.

To increase business through shorter journey times, using the new technical understanding but without building a new railway, was the problem to which the Advanced Passenger Train proved the answer. Using the tilt concept to allow speed to be maintained through curves, a lower centre of gravity and the use of new techniques for producing a lighter vehicle with a better profile, the idea offered sufficient promise for a government contribution to the development programme.

Four years of activity at Derby, where a new APT test hall was constructed, produced APT-E, a four-car embodiment of these dramatic new ideas and intended as a mobile test bed. APT-E started running on the test track and between 1972 and 1975 provided much essential information for the Research and Development team and for the CM&EE designers who had now become involved in the project. Gas turbines were used for propulsion because of the prohibitive weight of diesel

TRAIN EVOLUTION AND DESCRIPTION

engines and the train incorporated power tilting and hydrokinetic brakes.

While work on APT was progressing, further BR studies of the passenger market underlined the requirement for speed and made it clear that straight replacement of conventional trains would not retain, let alone increase, rail travel. The need for a better alternative was underlined and both the APT and HST projects received new impetus, the former being transferred from the research function to the designers in 1972.

Gas turbines had not proved satisfactory in APT-E and axlehung motors now gave way to thyristor-controlled traction equipment based on two power cars. Each has two four-wheel bogies and four 750 kW body-mounted traction motors. The motors drive the axles via a body-mounted gearbox. Within a very tight weight specification the eventual design produced equipment capable of a continuous rated traction output of 3,000 kW plus 760 kW of auxiliary power.

The change from APT-E to APT-P coincided with a breakthrough in the production of long aluminium extrusions. Using these in place of the former riveted construction with a light alloy skin produced dividends for the trailer cars, the power cars remaining of steel.

To avoid high power cabling through the train or an over concentration of power, APT-P comprises two power cars in the centre with two six-car articulated trailer sets marshalled either side, in effect two trains back to back as passengers may not pass through the power cars in normal circumstances. Weighing 69 tonnes, the power cars are semi-monocoque assemblies in lightweight steel and with deep side skirts.

By using aluminium alloy a weight saving of some 40% was achieved in the trailer cars. As high flexural natural frequencies are essential for good riding qualities at high speeds the increase in 'stiffness' was another dividend. The six cars are articulated but the ball joint articulation of the APT-E design has given way to structurally separate cars which ride on long bogies provided at each end with a yoke to carry the secondary air springs and with hydraulic rams for tilting. Built to UIC loading specifications, including a 200 tonne proof buffing load, the passenger vehicles are of three basic types with kitchen/ buffet/restaurant facilities duplicated in each rake.

Perhaps the most revolutionary feature of the Advanced Passenger Train is the tilting provision. By shaping the vehicle bodies a tilt of 9° is possible within the loading gauge and is derived from hydraulic jacks acting on a rotating bolster within the bogie frame. A twin pump system provides pressure for low and high speed tilting which is controlled electronically by measurement of the lateral acceleration of the bolster, electrical connections sensing the 'spirit level bubble' in the accelerometer. In the event of failure, the vehicle bodies return to an upright position.

The standard pantograph has been improved for current collection at high speeds but this, of course, does not tilt with the vehicle. An anti-tilt linkage isolates the pantograph from lateral movements and a medium stiffness roll bar is provided. Only one pantograph is raised at a time to give good current collection at high speeds.

The traction motors drive the APT power car axles via a body-mounted gearbox, cardan shaft and lightweight final reduction gearbox. The power cars have BP17a bogies with four large helical springs enclosing viscous dampers. The two types of trailer bogies (BT12 for the end trailer and BT11 for intermediate articulated positions) have helical spring primary suspension and air spring secondary suspension. The trailer wheelsets can be exchanged without lifting the body.

The APT concept called for the minimum changes in signalling as well as in track considerations. This in turn demanded a low-weight, high retardation braking system capable of coping with retardation levels up to 0.14g. The hydrokinetic solution is based on a stator and rotor enclosed in a chamber and between which a water-glycol mixture creates a restraining torque during the braking process. Friction brakes take over as speed decreases. Driver control is exercised by means of an electrically coded signal translated at the axle through an electro-pneumatic valve into reservoir pressure and thus braking rate.

Internally, the Advanced Passenger Train offers a high standard of passenger comfort. Despite a slight loss of length and width in the overall dimensions, the use of two door vestibules has maintained a saloon length comparable with the Mark III coach and careful design has preserved seating space. There is provision for 72 second class seats arranged 2 + 2 with tables between and 47 first class seats, 2 + 1 wide, again with tables and also with variable sitting positions.

Fluorescent lighting with a minimum illumination level of 240 lux. is housed in diffuser panels and there is full air conditioning. The latter is based on 24 kW of heating in three stages and 25 kW of cooling power in an under-floor refrigeration unit and working in two stages. To conserve energy, a recurring APT theme, only 15% of the circulated air is taken in through the transient pressure protection valves the remainder being recycled in its filter/ceiling/input to filter/floor/output progression. A maximum noise level of 76 dBB has been achieved by a mixture of good design, flexible mountings, damping compounds and air insulation. Seats, luggage racks and other such items are attractively designed and easy to service. Chemical toilets of advanced design are incorporated.

Cab layout in the Advanced Passenger Train is similar to that in the HSTs. The nose of the cab can be raised to expose retractable buffers and a drophead coupler of the buckeye type and with drawhook. Behind the driver the standby diesel alternator and 110 v battery are housed while the motor alternator set for power and air supplies to auxiliary equipment is adjacent to the guard and parcels accommodation at the other end of the set.

After authority to build three pre-production prototype APTs was given in October 1974 work started on the first unit at BREL's Derby Locomotive Works and the first vehicle, one of the six power cars, emerged in June 1977. It was soon on main line test, joined in 1978 by the first trailer cars. By 1979 a second APT-P was in use for driver training and in 1980 the Minister of Transport made an inaugural journey.

Since the design period around 1973 energy costs generally have risen steeply. Although APT-P is capable of more than 150 mph (and effectively demonstrated this on test on 20 December 1979) the higher energy costs resulting would reduce some of the advantages of the project. With a 125 mph limitation, braking distances are similar to those of locomotive hauled services so that costly modifications to the signalling system can be avoided. On curves, despite the higher speeds, a 17 tonne axleload limit and a suspension that minimises the flange contact reduces track forces to the same as those exerted by the existing electric services.

The commencement of revenue-earning operation by the Advanced Passenger Train in 1981 is only one more step in the dramatic BR development programme. With a capital cost very similar to that of the HST and a running cost 35% lower the plan is to incorporate the further experience that timetabled running will provide into an expansion of the APT activity until it eventually handles all the daytime main line services out of Euston. Calling for around sixty trains in all, each intensively utilised, such a development would allow optimisation of line capacity based on grouping trains in similar speed bands.

The production APTs will embrace a new design of power car. Speeds of 125 – 130 mph, which are commercially acceptable, will permit the use of a form-ation based on one power car and ten trailers, thus eliminating the need to duplicate catering facilities.

For the passenger the Advanced Passenger Train will provide a smooth, fast and congenial ride without the payment of special supplements and giving excellent value for money. And if the case for further main line electrification is accepted, by the end of the 1980s APT could be serving other routes where curves are at present the restraining factor.

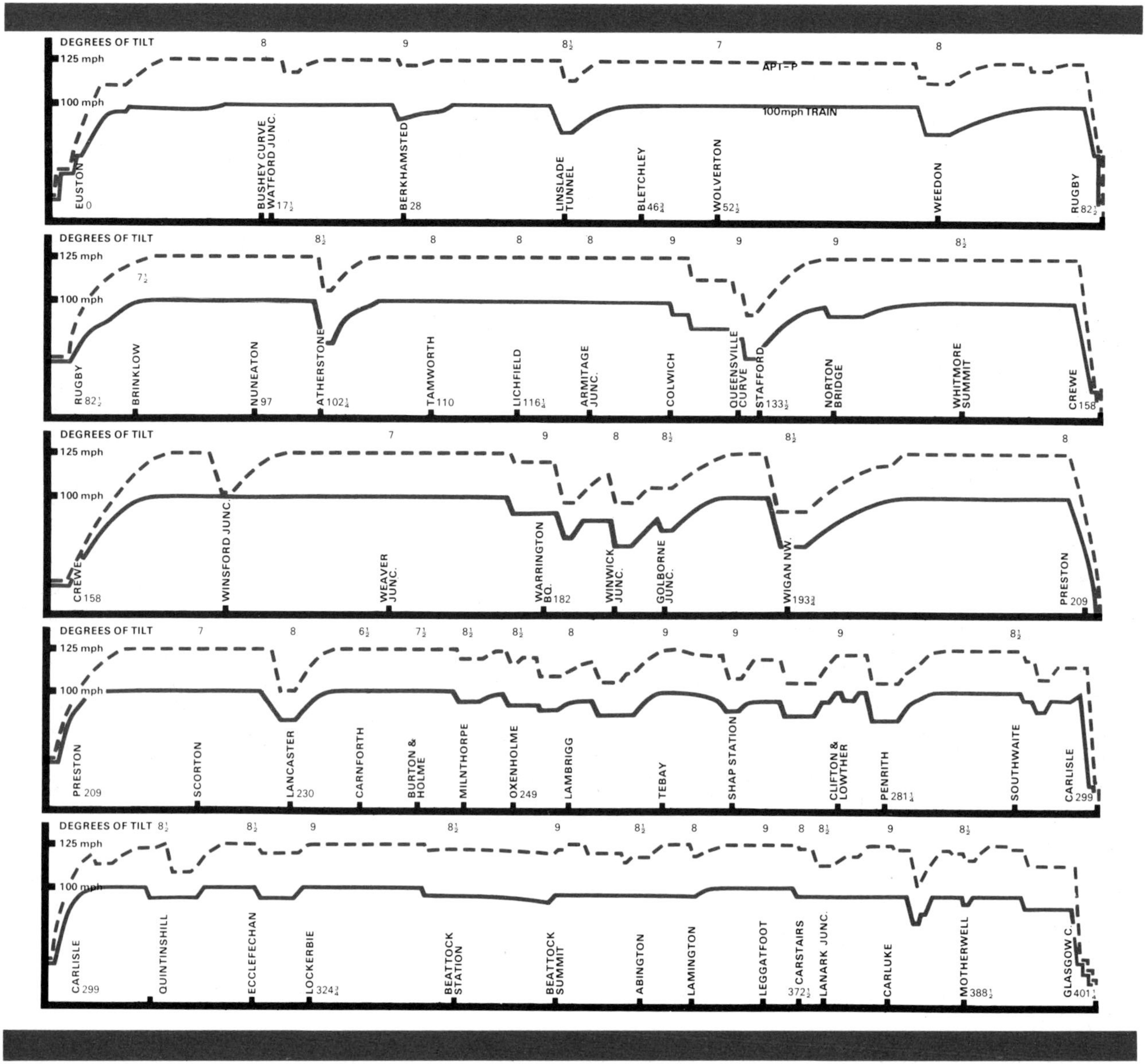

DEGREES OF TILT
8
9
8½
7
8
125 mph
100 mph
APT–P
100mph TRAIN
EUSTON 0
BUSHEY CURVE
WATFORD JUNC. 17½
BERKHAMSTED 28
LINSLADE TUNNEL
BLETCHLEY 46¾
WOLVERTON 52½
WEEDON
RUGBY 82½
DEGREES OF TILT
8½
8
8
8
9
9
9
8½
7½
125 mph
100 mph
RUGBY 82½
BRINKLOW
NUNEATON 97
ATHERSTONE 102¼
TAMWORTH 110
LICHFIELD 116¼
ARMITAGE JUNC.
COLWICH
QUEENSVILLE CURVE
STAFFORD 133½
NORTON BRIDGE
WHITMORE SUMMIT
CREWE 158
DEGREES OF TILT
7
9
8
8½
8½
8
125 mph
100 mph
CREWE 158
WINSFORD JUNC.
WEAVER JUNC.
WARRINGTON BQ. 182
WINWICK JUNC.
GOLBORNE JUNC.
WIGAN NW. 193¾
PRESTON 209
DEGREES OF TILT
7
8
6½
7½
8½
8½
8
9
9
9
8½
125 mph
100 mph
PRESTON 209
SCORTON
LANCASTER 230
CARNFORTH
BURTON & HOLME
MILNTHORPE
OXENHOLME 249
LAMBRIGG
TEBAY
SHAP STATION
CLIFTON & LOWTHER
PENRITH 281¼
SOUTHWAITE
CARLISLE 299
DEGREES OF TILT
8½
8½
9
8½
9
8½
8
9
8
8½
9
8½
125 mph
100 mph
CARLISLE 299
QUINTINSHILL
ECCLEFECHAN
LOCKERBIE 324¾
BEATTOCK STATION
BEATTOCK SUMMIT
ABINGTON
LAMINGTON
LEGGATFOOT
CARSTAIRS 372½
LANARK JUNC.
CARLUKE
MOTHERWELL 388½
GLASGOW C. 401¼

The Advanced Passenger Train stands in Euston station. Ahead lies the 401¼ mile route to Glasgow serving the Midlands and North West and then rising steeply at 1 in 75 on the climb to Shap Summit before dropping again to Carlisle and the border. There is now a further 102½ miles, and another stiff climb of 10 miles from Beattock up to the summit there, before the line starts the long descent towards Glasgow and the Clyde. The chart opposite shows the main points along the route, with an unbroken line for the speed graph of ordinary trains and a broken line denoting the APT schedule. Degrees of tilt are also shown.

PLANS DRAWINGS AND DIAGRAMS

1 Pantograph.
2 Circuit Breaker.
3 H.T. Bus-Bar.
4 Gangway Connection.
5 Drawbar.
6 Hydrokinetic Brake Radiator and Fan.
7 Hydrokinetic Brake Air Reservoir.
8 Hydrokinetic Brake Water Reservoir.
9 Door.
10 Pantograph Anti-tilt Mechanism.
11 Hydrokinetic Brake Controls.
12 Hydrokinetic Brake.
13 Transmission Gearbox.
14 Traction Motor & Blower.
15 Electric Control Equipment
16 Air Compressor.
17 Cooling Fan for Transformer, Choke, Thyristor and Tilt systems.
18 Thyristor Convertors.
19 Choke.
20 Radiators for Transformer, Choke, Thyristors and Tilt Systems.
21 Thyristor Coolant Tank and Pump.
22 Transformer.
23 Batteries.
24 Tilt System Control Pack.
25 Fire Extinguisher Gas Bottles.
26 Ventilation Fan.

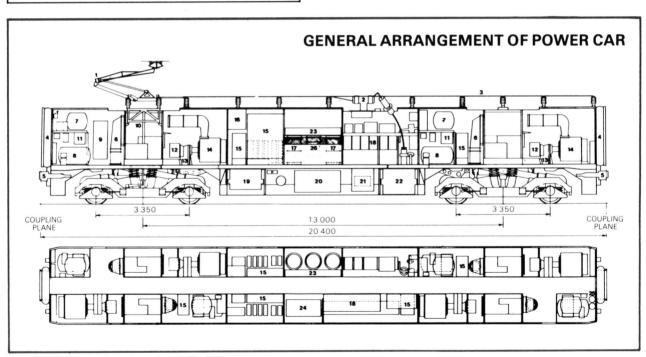

GENERAL ARRANGEMENT OF POWER CAR

COUPLING PLANE   3 350   13 000   3 350   COUPLING PLANE
20 400

LAYOUT OF APT-P VEHICLES

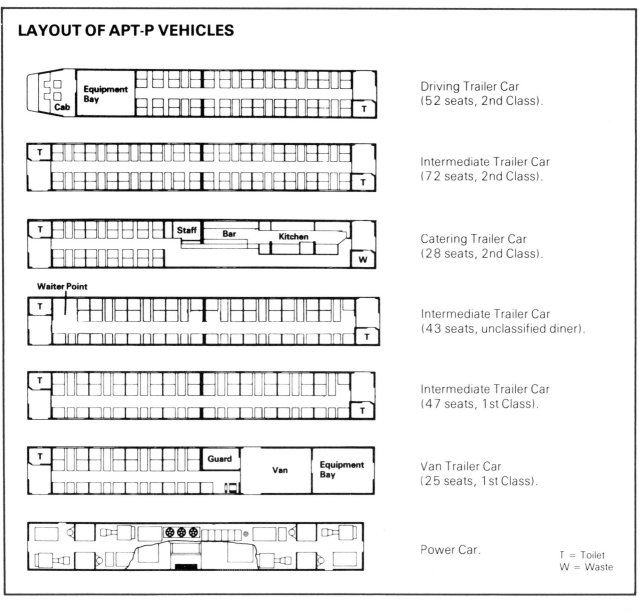

Driving Trailer Car
(52 seats, 2nd Class).

Intermediate Trailer Car
(72 seats, 2nd Class).

Catering Trailer Car
(28 seats, 2nd Class).

Intermediate Trailer Car
(43 seats, unclassified diner).

Intermediate Trailer Car
(47 seats, 1st Class).

Van Trailer Car
(25 seats, 1st Class).

Power Car.

T = Toilet
W = Waste

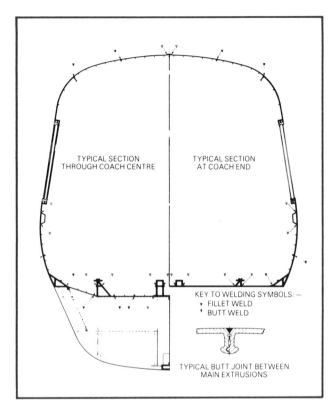

TYPICAL SECTION
THROUGH COACH CENTRE

TYPICAL SECTION
AT COACH END

KEY TO WELDING SYMBOLS:—
▽ FILLET WELD
▾ BUTT WELD

TYPICAL BUTT JOINT BETWEEN
MAIN EXTRUSIONS

APT TRAILER CAR STRUCTURE

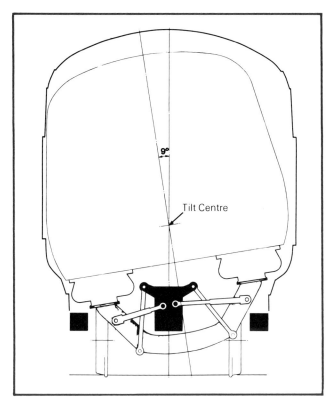

9°

Tilt Centre

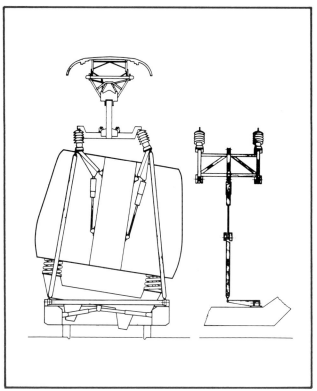

APT TILT SUSPENSION

**APT PANTOGRAPH
ANTI-TILT MECHANISM**

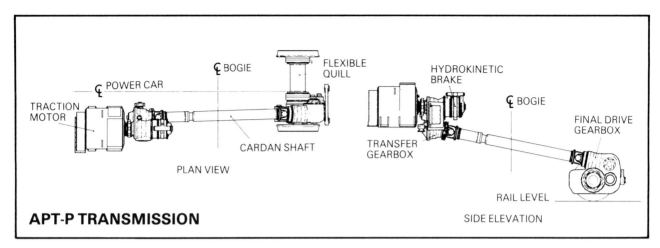

TRACTION MOTOR

POWER CAR

BOGIE

FLEXIBLE QUILL

CARDAN SHAFT

PLAN VIEW

HYDROKINETIC BRAKE

BOGIE

FINAL DRIVE GEARBOX

TRANSFER GEARBOX

RAIL LEVEL

SIDE ELEVATION

APT-P TRANSMISSION

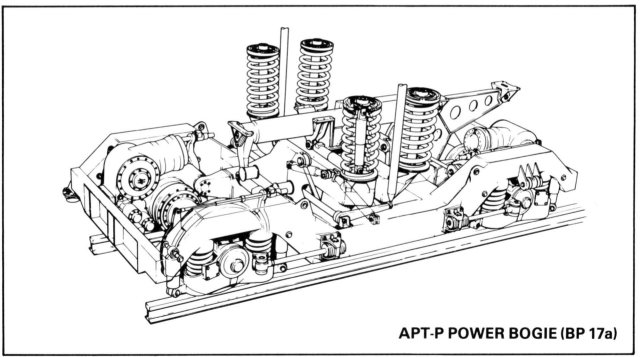

APT-P POWER BOGIE (BP 17a)

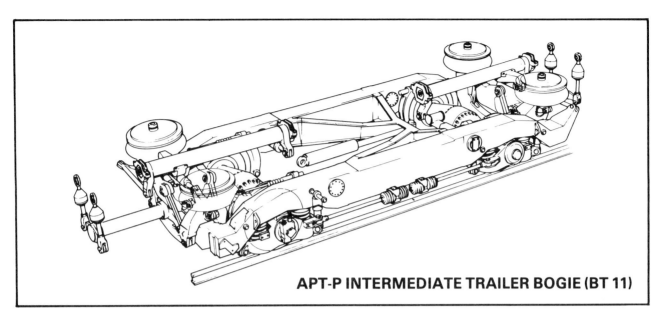

APT-P INTERMEDIATE TRAILER BOGIE (BT 11)

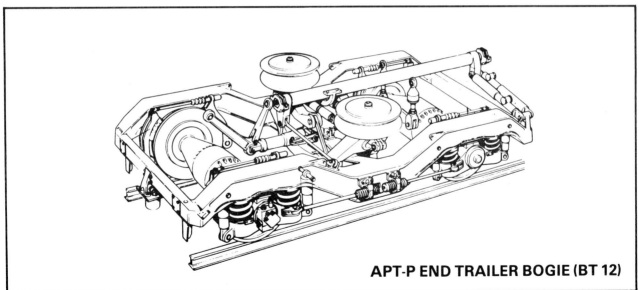

APT-P END TRAILER BOGIE (BT 12)

APT-P CONSTRUCTION

Opposite, various stages of body construction are depicted; and, *on this page,* bogies, pantograph, air suspension bag and completed power car.

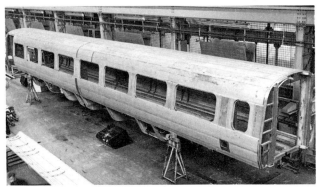 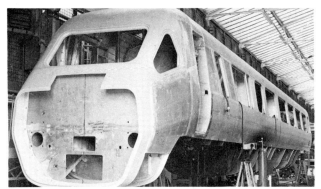

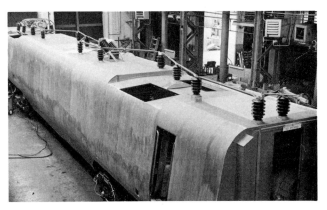 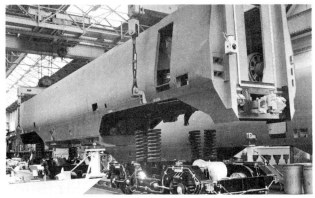

ADVANCED PASSENGER TRAIN *in Action*

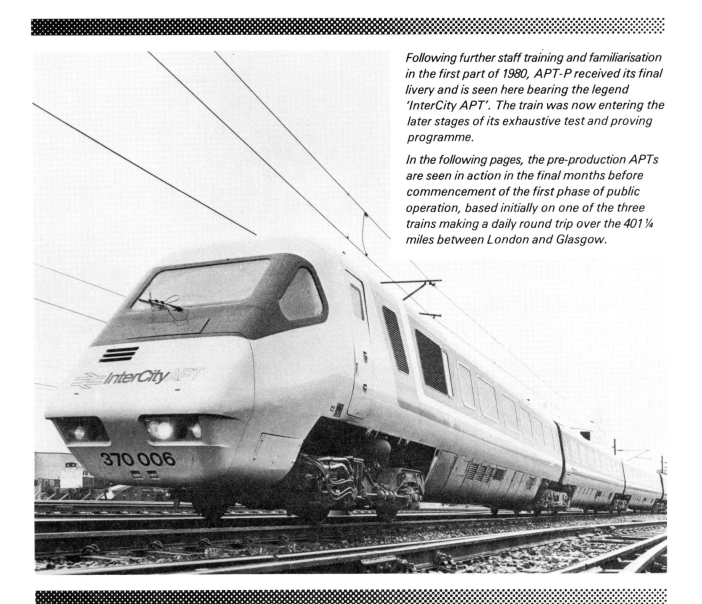

Following further staff training and familiarisation in the first part of 1980, APT-P received its final livery and is seen here bearing the legend 'InterCity APT'. The train was now entering the later stages of its exhaustive test and proving programme.

In the following pages, the pre-production APTs are seen in action in the final months before commencement of the first phase of public operation, based initially on one of the three trains making a daily round trip over the 401¼ miles between London and Glasgow.

APT–P
at Preston

In the rain at Preston APT-P shows its clean lines and the spacious door openings, as well as exciting the interest of young admirers.

APT-P *at Beattock*

The driver's console in APT-P makes interesting comparison with the APT-E layout depicted on page 13. This view shows clearly the C-APT advisory system which provides an automatic digital visual display of the higher speed limits applicable to APT trains and which is derived from transponder track beacons.

The streamlined nose cone of the APT end units can be raised to allow coupling to conventional locomotives for movement in emergencies or over non-electrified sections. This view shows the buckeye-type coupler, buffing gear and standard train pipe connections.

Full refreshment facilities are provided in the Advanced Passenger Trains. In APT-P a bar and buffet service and a full meal service are offered and the main kitchen in each 'set' is located between the two facilities. As this view shows, the kitchens are modern, spacious and fully equipped.

Modern, well-designed equipment is also provided for Advanced Passenger Train guards. It includes a train broadcasting facility for providing journey information. The guard's 'office', which includes direct communication with the driver, is located in the trailer vehicle next to the power car.

The APT-P design provides for fast and efficient maintenance. The scene above demonstrates the method of removing the bogies, while the illustrations opposite show the unit component principle applied to the underfloor equipment. The air-conditioned car interior is light and attractive with seats designed for maximum comfort and upholstered in tartan, as pictured on the far right.

The Advanced Passenger Train is a revolutionary piece of railway engineering of which British Rail is rightly proud. It owes its success to an imaginative concept, untiring research and design effort and to skilled engineering and operational contributions. The role of the APT, as these scenes remind us, is to enable passengers to travel faster and in maximum comfort.

APT-E Project

Nov 1966	'High Speed' study team formed in Research Department.
1967	Concept of high performance tilting train developed.
Feb 1968	Basic proposals for APT formulated.
Jan 1969	Experimental APT-E project authorised.
1970–71	Design and construction of 2-car APT-POP train and 4-car, gas turbine powered APT-E.
Sep 1971	Track testing of APT-POP commenced.
Jul 1972	First test run of APT-E on main line.
Dec 1974	10,000 miles of test running completed.
Aug 1975	Speed of 152 mph reached between Swindon and Reading.
Oct 1975	Test run from St Pancras to Leicester in 58½ minutes at an average speed of 101.5 mph.
Apr 1976	Last test run — 23,560 miles completed. APT-E retired to National Railway Museum, York.

APT-P Project

Jan 1973	Responsibility for APT transferred from Head of Research to Chief Mechanical & Electrical Engineer.
Apr 1973	Joint Review Team submitted design proposals for APT-P.
Oct 1973	Design work approved.
Sep 1974	APT-P project authorised for three trains.
Jan 1976	Power car construction commenced.
Jun 1977	First power car delivered.
Sep 1977	Track testing of power car test train initiated.
Oct 1977	Power car ran at 125 mph under its own power.
Jun 1978	First rake of trailer cars delivered.
Jul 1978	Track testing of trailer rake test train initiated.
Feb 1979	First train APT—1 based at Glasgow for proving trials.
Apr 1979	APT—1 makes its first run from Shields Depot under its own power.
May 1979	Primary series of track proving trials started.
Dec 1979	APT—1 reaches a maximum speed of 160 mph at Lockerbie. Second train APT—2 formed and started driver training.
Feb 1980	APT—1 stood down on successful completion of primary trials.
Sep 1980	Minister of Transport travels on APT.
Oct 1980	Train demonstrated to the Press.

ORDER FORM

To Avon-AngliA Publications & Services, Annesley House, 21 Southside, Weston-super-Mare, Avon BS23 2QU.

Please send me the items ticked below:

LIVERPOOL & MANCHESTER: A Photographic Essay. The official B.R. record of the 1980 Rainhill Cavalcade. Price £1.65 _____

ROCKET 150. The Liverpool & Manchester Railway 1830—1980. BR Official Handbook. Price £2.40 _____

INVICTA 150—Canterbury & Whitstable Railway: A Pioneer Line and the area it served. Price £1.50 _____

Canterbury & Whitstable: Special Commemorative Collection of historic items. Price £10 _____

Riviera Express — The Train and Its Route. Price 95p _____

Paddington 1854—1979. An illustrated history of Brunel's famous London terminus. Price £1 _____

Rail 125 in Action. HST diagrams, data and action pictures. price 60p _____

Clinker's Register of Closed Stations and Goods Depots in England, Scotland & Wales 1830—1977. 10,000 entries, 27,000 dates, 4,000 notes. Price £8.50 _____

Supplement No. 1 to Clinker's Register. Price £1 _____

GWR: A Register of Halts & Platforms 1903—1979. Price £1.75 _____

Leicester & Swannington Railway. A detailed history of the poineer line of the Midlands. Price £2.50 _____

The Ashby-de-la-Zouch Canal and its Railways. Price 95p _____

Signalling — From Mechanics to Modules. Price 90p _____

Bristol & North Somerset Railway Vol. 1 1863—1884. Price 75p _____

Bristol & North Somerset Railway Vol. 2. Since 1884. Price £1.25 _____

Severn & Wye Joint Lines. 1923 map and historical notes. Price 90p _____

New Light on the Gauge Conversion A detailed account of a remarkable piece of railway history. Price £1 _____

Wrington Vale Light Railway. A branch line history. Price 95p _____

East Somerset Railway 1858—1972 Price 70p _____

Ellesmere Port — Canal Town. The Shropshire Union Canal and the town it created. Price 80p _____

Triumph of the Royal Scot. Reprint of the 1933 North American Tour booklet. Price 80p _____

Railway History Sources. Price £1 _____

Light Railway Orders. Price £1.50 _____

Clifton Suspension Bridge. The full and fascinating history of Brunel's bridge. Price £3.50 _____

Clearwell Castle Story. The story of a D.I.Y. drama. price 50p _____

Bristol Avon Railway. The Bath to Mangotsfield line and the Bitton Railway Centre. Price 70p _____

Western Railtourist: The West Country. The official BR (WR) guide to the counties of the West in pack of special items. Price £1.50 _____

NEW TITLES

Guide to Light Railways, Canals, Steamers & Industrial Preservation. Data on several hundred locations and activities. Price 90p _____

Railways on Record. Details all known LP and 45 rpm British railway sounds. Price £7.50 _____

Rail Data Book: A Modern Railway Companion. A wealth of British rail facts and information. Price 95p _____

Advanced Passenger Train: The official book of BR's 155 mph train, with 72 special photographs and illustrations. £1.95 _____

Western at Work Series:
No. 1 British Rail's Western Region. Price £1.25 _____

No. 2 Western Motive Power. £1.40 _____

No. 3 Heart of Wales Line. 85p _____

Remittance enclosed for _____
Please add 15% for postage and packing on all orders of less than £5.

S.A.E. and tick as required for: —
Out-of-print, booklet and other specialist items list ☐

Details of our Transport Publications Circle ☐

ADDRESS _____
_____
_____
_____